ORACLE (1Z0-2
PEOPLESOFT APPLICATION DEVELOPER II -
APPLICATION ENGINE & INTEGRATION
EXAM PRACTICE QUESTIONS & DUMPS

100+ Exam practice questions for Oracle 1Z0-242 updated 2020

Presented By: Emerald Books

About Emerald Books:

Emerald Books is a publishing house based in Hudson, Texas, USA, a platform that is available both online & locally, which unleashes the power of educational content, literary collection, poetry & many other book genres. We make it easy for writers & authors to get their books designed, published, promoted, and sell professionally on worldwide scale with eBook + Print distribution. Emerald Books was founded in 2015, and is now distributing books worldwide.

QUESTION 1

Evaluate this PeopleCode snippet. Local Array of Number &MyArray; Local Any &Len, &Result; &MyArray = CreateArray(3);

&MyArray[1] = 100;

&MyArray[2] = 200;

&MyArray[3] = 300;

&Result = &MyArray.POP(); &Len = &MyArray.LEN; &End = &MyArray[&Len];
What are the correct values for &Result and &End?

A. &Result is 300 &End is 200
B. &Result is 300 &End is Null
C. &Result is 300 &End is 300
D. &Result is Null &End is 300
E. &Result is 100 &End is 300

Correct Answer: A

QUESTION 2

Here is a snippet of PeopleCode that uses the Fetch method of the SQL class.

&SQL = CreateSQL("Select EFFORT_AMT from PS_PSU_TASK_EFFORT where TASK= :1", PSU_TASK_TBL.TASK);
&Var1 = &SQL.Fetch(&Var2);

Select the two correct statements. (Choose two.)

A. &Var2 specifies which row to fetch.
B. &Var2 specifies which field to fetch.
C. &Var1 is populated with TRUE if a row is fetched.
D. &Var1 is populated with the number of rows returned.
E. &Var2 is populated with EFFORT_AMT from the row fetched.
F. &Var1 is populated with EFFORT_AMT from the row fetched.
G. &Var1 is populated with EFFORT_AMT from the first row returned.

Correct Answer: CE

QUESTION 3

View the Exhibit.

An object-oriented PeopleCode program traverses the data buffer to get the value for Session Number (SESSION_NBR) in the Session Details record (PSU_CRS_SESSN) on the Course Sessions page.
The program uses a built-in function to instantiate the Level 0 object, then uses object methods to instantiate the remaining data buffer objects.

Select the option that represents the order in which the program instantiates the data buffer objects.

A. &Row_Level0, &Row_Level1, &Record, &Field
B. &Rowset_Level0, &Row_Level1, &Record, &Field
C. &Rowset_Level0, &Rowset_Level1, &Row_Level1, &Record, &Field
D. &Rowset_Level0, &Row_Level0, &Rowset_Level1, &Row_Level1, &Record, &Field

Correct Answer: D

QUESTION 4

The Customer Orders page uses data from the ITEM table to perform price calculations. You decide to write a PeopleCode program to create a stand-alone rowset that will load data from the ITEM table into the data buffer. Select three PeopleCode statements that can be used with stand-alone rowsets. (Choose three.)

A. &RS_Item = GetRowSet(SCROLL.ITEM);
B. &RS_Item = CreateRowSet(RECORD.ITEM);
C. &Price = &RS_Item(&i).ITEM.PRICE.Value;
D. &RS_Item.Select("Where ITEM = :1", CUST_ORDER.ITEM);
E. &RS_Item.Fill("Where CUST_TYPE = :1", CUST_ORDER.TYPE);
F. &RS_Item = ScrollSelect(1,Scroll.ITEM, Record.ITEM, ("Where CUST_TYPE = :1", CUST_ORDER. CUST_TYPE);

Correct Answer: BCE

QUESTION 5

The Application Engine program PSU_PROC_CRSE has a Do Select action with the following code:

%Select (COURSE, EFFDT, DESCR, TOOLS_REL) SELECT COURSE , EFFDT

, DESCR

, TOOLS_REL

FROM PS_PSU_COURSE_TBL A
WHERE A.EFFDT <= (SELECT MAX(A1.EFFDT) FROM PS_PSU_COURSE_TBL A1
WHERE A1.COURSE = A.COURSE AND A1.EFFDT <= GETDATE())

The program works fine in testing, but it fails when run on an Oracle database platform.

Select the two approaches that will resolve the problem and give the expected results. (Choose two.)

A. Delete the Where clause.
B. Change the WHERE clause to WHERE A.EFFDT = MAX(EFFDT).
C. Change the SELECT clause to SELECT DISTINCT.
D. Change the WHERE clause to WHERE %EffdtCheck(PSU_COURSE_TBL A, %CurrentDateIn).
E. Replace the GETDATE() function with the %CurrentDateIn system variable.

F. Select the Active check box on the step so that the PeopleSoft Application Engine automatically selects the current row.

Correct Answer: DE

QUESTION 6

On the Service Operation definition page, the Introspection link is used to_____

A. provide a Web service
B. consume a Web service
C. add a new service operation
D. add a new service operation version
E. add routing to existing service operation

Correct Answer: E

QUESTION 7

If Review Type is Peer or Performance, then the prompt for Reviewer ID returns all employees. Select the three steps required to implement this business rule. (Choose three.)

A. Associate the REVIEWER_ID field with REVIEWER_VW.
B. Create REVIEWER_VW as a dynamic view of the EMPLOYEE table.
C. Add the DERIVED.EDITTABLE field to the page and make it invisible.
D. Set the prompt table edit for the REVIEWER_ID field to REVIEWER_VW.
E. Set the prompt table edit for the REVIEWER_ID field to DERIVED.%EDITTABLE.
F. Use a SQL Select statement in PeopleCode to populate the REVIEWER_VW view.
G. Use a conditional statement in PeopleCode to populate the DERIVED.EDITTABLE field.

Correct Answer: CEG

QUESTION 8

You want to examine the component buffer for the Customer Orders
(PSU_CUST_ORDER) component. Which four steps are necessary? (Choose
four.)

A. Start the PeopleCode Debugger and set a breakpoint.
B. Access the Structure view on the PSU_CUST_ORDER component.
C. In Application Designer, select Component Buffers.
D. Access the Customer Orders component in the browser and trigger the
   breakpoint. Return to PeopleSoft Application Designer when the breakpoint
   triggers.

E. Open, or create, a PeopleCode program that will execute while Customer
   Orders is running in the browser.
F. Drill down through the component hierarchy in the Structure view on the
   PSU_CUST_ORDER component.
G. In Application Designer, select Debug, View Component Buffers.

Correct Answer: ADEG

QUESTION 9

View the Exhibit.

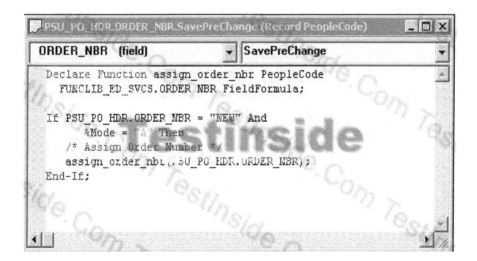

Your client is upgrading its purchasing application to use object-oriented PeopleCode to incorporate the benefits of application classes.

The PeopleCode for the Purchase Order application is now encapsulated in an Application Package called PSU_PO. The assign_order_nbr function is now ORDER_NBR, a method of the ORDER class.
You are tasked with modifying this program to call the new ORDER_NBR method. Which four PeopleCode statements will you use in the new program? (Choose four.)

A. Class PSU_PO:ORDER;
B. &New.ORDER_NBR(PSU_PO_HDR.ORDER_NBR);
C. Import PSU_PO:ORDER;
D. Declare method PSU_PO:ORDER:ORDER_NBR;
E. &New = Create Order();
F. Local ORDER &New;
G. Method ORDER_NBR (&ORDER_NBR As Field out);

Correct Answer: BCEF

QUESTION 10

You want to see exactly when a PeopleCode program fires in the context of the Component Processor flow. Which two methods will work? (Choose two.)

A. Insert a Print() statement in the program.
B. Insert a WinMessage() statement in the program.
C. Insert a MessageCatalog() statement in the program.
D. Run the PeopleCode Debugger and insert a breakpoint on the program.
E. Run the PeopleCode Debugger and select Debug, View Component Buffers.

Correct Answer: BD

QUESTION 11

View the Exhibit.

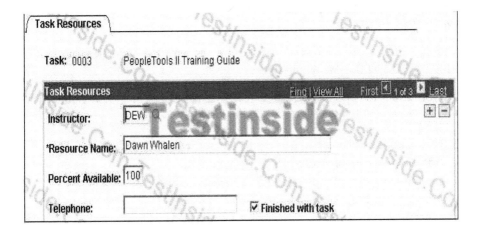

A PeopleCode program at level 0 checks the values for Percent Available (PCT_AVAILABLE) at level 1. Analyze this code snippet.
Local Rowset &RS_Level0, &RS_Level1; Local Row &Row_Level0, &Row_Level1; Local Record &Rec_TaskRsrc;
Local Field & Fld_PctAvail ;

&RS_Level0 = GetLevel0(); &Row_Level0 = &RS_Level0.GetRow(1);

&RS_Level1 = &Row_Level0.GetRowset(Scroll.PSU_TASK_RSRC);
&Row_Level1 = &RS_Level1.GetRow(1);

&Rec_TaskRsrc = &Row_Level1.GetRecord(Record.PSU_Task_RSRC);

&Fld_PctAvail = &Rec_TaskRsrc.GetField(Field.PCT_AVAILABLE); &Pct = &Fld_PctAvail.Value;
Select the correct option.

A. The program will produce the expected results.
B. The program is missing a loop to process each row in the level 1 rowset.
C. The program is missing a loop to process each rowset in the level 1 row.
D. The program can be simplified to:
    &Pct = &RS_Level0.PSU_Task_RSRC.PCT_AVAILABLE.Value;
E. This line of code is not needed:
    &RS_Level1 = &Row_Level0.GetRowset(Scroll.PSU_TASK_RSRC);
F. The &RS_Level0 = GetLevel0(); function is missing the Level 0 scroll name.

Correct Answer: B

QUESTION 12

The Get Student Enrollments page uses a PeopleCode program to select and display rows based on user input.

When the user clicks Refresh, FieldChange PeopleCode populates a stand-alone rowset using a Select method.

When you test the program, the new rows are appended to the previous rows instead of replacing them. How do you fix this problem?

A. Use a work scroll instead of a stand-alone rowset.
B. Add &Rowset.Flush(); after the Select method.
C. Use an Update method instead of a Select method.
D. Add &Rowset.Flush(); before the Select method.
E. Add &Rowset.Refresh (); after the Select method.
F. Add &Rowset.Refresh(); before the Select method.

Correct Answer: D

QUESTION 13

Examine the join in this Select statement:

SELECT A.TASK , B.EFFORT_AMT FROM PS_PROJECT A , PS_EFFORT B
WHERE A.TASK = B.TASK AND A.RESOURCE = B.RESOURCE

Select the equivalent Select statement.

A. SELECT A.TASK , B.EFFORT_AMT FROM PS_PROJECT A , PS_EFFORT
   B WHERE %Join(A.TASK, B.RESOURCE)
B. SELECT A.TASK , B.EFFORT_AMT FROM PS_PROJECT A , PS_EFFORT
   B
   WHERE %Common(PROJECT A, EFFORT B)
C. SELECT A.TASK , B.EFFORT_AMT
   FROM %Common(KEYS, PROJECT A, EFFORT B)
D. SELECT A.TASK , B.EFFORT_AMT FROM PS_PROJECT A , PS_EFFORT
   B
   WHERE %Join(COMMON_KEYS, TASK A, EFFORT_AMT B)
E. SELECT A.TASK , B.EFFORT_AMT
   FROM %Join(COMMON_KEYS, PROJECT A, EFFORT B)

Correct Answer: E

QUESTION 14

A Process Scheduler process is configured to run an Application Engine program. You need to modify the process to use parameters entered by the user at run time. Which four additional steps do you need to take? (Choose four.)

A. Create a process type for the new process.
B. Add bind variables to the command-line parameters.
C. Write a PeopleCode program to pass the parameters.
D. Create a state record with fields to pass input parameters.
E. Create a run control page with fields to enter the input parameters.
F. Create a run control record with fields to store the input parameters.
G. Modify the Application Engine program to retrieve the input parameters.

Correct Answer: DEFG

QUESTION 15

View the Exhibit.

This run control page executes an Application Engine program that updates the Course table using the parameters entered by a user.

In addition to the run control page, which three elements must be in place? (Choose three.)

A. A state record with fields to hold input parameters
B. Component variables to pass the input parameters
C. A data buffer object to retrieve the input parameters
D. Application Engine SQL to retrieve the input parameters
E. A PeopleCode record object to update the Course table
F. A Process Instance table to store run control parameters

G. A run control record with fields to store the input parameters

Correct Answer: ADG

QUESTION 16

Select three Application Engine action types that can be used to control program flow. (Choose three.)

A. Log Message
B. Call Section
C. XSLT
D. PeopleCode
E. Do While
F. Evaluate

Correct Answer: BDE

QUESTION 17

You modify an Application Engine program to use parallel processing with temporary tables. The Application Engine program includes this code snippet, which is part of a SQL statement that inserts rows into a temporary table.

INSERT INTO PS_CRS_FULL_TMP

What changes do you need to make to the code so that the Application Engine program will implement parallel processing properly?

A. No changes to the code are needed as long as the temporary table has been properly configured for parallel processing.
B. Replace INSERT INTO PS_CRS_FULL_TMP with %INSERT INTO PS_CRS_FULL_TMP so that the meta- SQL resolves to the correct state record at run time.
C. Replace INSERT INTO PS_CRS_FULL_TMP with %INSERT INTO %Table(CRS_FULL_TMP) so that the system variables resolve to the correct syntax at run time.
D. Replace INSERT INTO PS_CRS_FULL_TMP with INSERT INTO %Table(CRS_FULL_TMP) so that the meta-SQL resolves to the correct temporary table instance at run time.
E. Replace INSERT INTO PS_CRS_FULL_TMP with %INSERT INTO %Temp(CRS_FULL_TMP) so that the meta-SQL resolves to the correct syntax and temporary table instance at run time.

Correct Answer: D

QUESTION 18

An Application Engine program uses a Do Select action. What occurs when the Select statement is executed?

A. Each row returned by the Select statement is stored in the state record. The Select statement continues until no more rows are returned. Then, the control passes to the calling section.

B. All rows returned by the Select statement are stored in a cursor. Then, the control is passed to the calling section.

C. All rows returned by the Select statement are stored in the state record. Then, the control is passed to the next section in the program.

D. All rows returned by the Select statement are stored in a cursor. The first row is stored in the state record. Then, the remaining actions in the step are processed sequentially. Thereafter, the control returns to the Do Select to fetch another row, until no more rows are returned.

E. When a row is returned, the remaining steps in the section execute and control returns to the calling step.

F. When a row is returned, it is stored in the state record. Then, the control is passed to the calling section.

Correct Answer: D

QUESTION 19

An Application Engine program inserts rows into PS_VENDOR. The program encounters an error and abends (ends abnormally).
You correct the error, but now PS_VENDOR is in an unknown state. Select the correct statement.

A. If Log File was enabled in Configuration Manager, a script file was created that you use to return the database to its original state. After you correct the error, you can run the program again.

B. If Recover was enabled for the program, the changes to PS_VENDOR are rolled back. After you correct the error, you can run the program again.

C. If Restart was enabled for the program, a checkpoint was saved with the last commit. After you correct the error, you can restart the program and processing will resume from the point of the last commit.

D. If Resume was enabled in PeopleSoft Process Scheduler, the program automatically resumes processing after the condition that caused the error is corrected.

E. If a state record was defined for the program, PS_VENDOR is restored based on parameters that were written to the state record. Then you can restart the program using the same run control parameters.

Correct Answer: C

QUESTION 20

How do you configure Process Scheduler to initiate an Application Engine trace for SQL and Step?

A. Add %%TRACE%% %%SQL%% %%STEP%% to the parameter list for the Process Type.
B. On the Run Control page, select the SQL Trace and Step Trace check boxes.
C. On the Process Monitor page, select the SQL Trace and Step Trace check boxes.
D. On the Process Definition Override Options page, for Parameter List, select Append and enter -TRACE 3.
E. On the Process Definition Override Options page, for Parameter List, select Append and enter -TRACE SQL STEP.
F. On the Process Definition Override Options page, for Parameter List, select Append and enter %%TRACE
    %% %%SQL%% %%STEP%%.

Correct Answer: D

QUESTION 21

,
WHERE a.ITEM_CD = b.ITEM_CD

You copy and paste the SQL statement to a Do Select action, but it needs to be modified so that it populates the PSU_ORDERS_AET state record. What do you need to do?

A. Change line 1 to:
    %SELECT a.ORDER_LINE_NBR
B. Add this line before line 1:
    INSERT INTO PS_PSU_ORDERS_AET
C. Add this line before line 1:
    %SELECT (ORDER_LINE_NBR, ITEM_CD, QTY_ORDERED, QTY_ON_HAND)
D. Add this line before line 1:
    %UPDATE (ORDER_LINE_NBR, ITEM_CD, QTY_ORDERED, QTY_ON_HAND)
E. Add this line after line 7:
    %INSERT (ORDER_LINE_NBR, ITEM_CD, QTY_ORDERED, QTY_ON_HAND)

Correct Answer: C

View the Exhibit, which shows Code Set Values. You will be using these code set values for the ORDER_STATUS field between System A (sender) and System B (recipient).

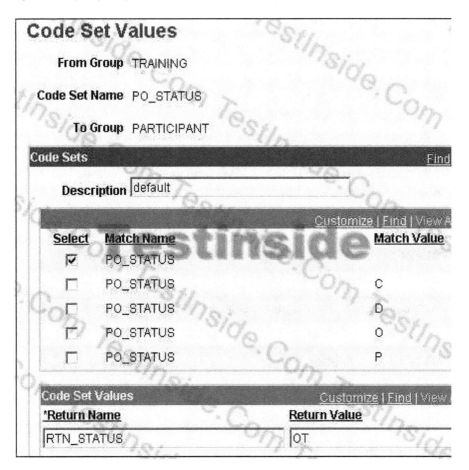

Which code set group, based on the data displayed in the exhibit, needs to be associated with System A?

A. TRAINING
B. PO_STATUS
C. PARTICIPANT
D. RTN_STATUS

Correct Answer: A

QUESTION 23

Here is a snippet of PeopleCode that uses the Fetch method of the SQL class.

&SQL = CreateSQL("Select EFFORT_AMT from PS_PSU_TASK_EFFORT where TASK= :1", PSU_TASK_TBL.TASK);
&Var1 = &SQL.Fetch(&Var2);

Select the two correct statements. (Choose two.)

A. &Var2 specifies which row to fetch.
B. &Var2 specifies which field to fetch.
C. &Var1 is populated with TRUE if a row is fetched.
D. &Var1 is populated with the number of rows returned.
E. &Var2 is populated with EFFORT_AMT from the row fetched.
F. &Var1 is populated with EFFORT_AMT from the row fetched.
G. &Var1 is populated with EFFORT_AMT from the first row returned.

Correct Answer: CE

QUESTION 24

An inbound request to a PeopleSoft application is received by the appropriate listening connector in the Integration Gateway. Which connector is the request passed to?

A. HTTP target connector
B. PeopleSoft target connector
C. PeopleSoft listening connector
D. PeopleSoft service listening connector

Correct Answer: B

QUESTION 25

An Application Engine batch program processes one million credit card transactions. The program takes four hours to complete. You have been tasked with reducing that time to two hours. You decide to use parallel processing because with parallel processing_____.

A. you effectively double your network bandwidth
B. you can distribute processing to multiple database servers
C. you reduce network traffic by transferring SQL processing to the database engine

D. you can run the program asynchronously instead of synchronously and reduce database table contention
E. you can divide the job into several sets of transactions, and process each set using different temporary tables

Correct Answer: E

QUESTION 26

Following the PeopleCode action, add a Call Section action. Select the correct statement

.

A. The Application Engine program will execute as expected.
B. Step 2 is not needed for dynamic call.
C. Step 3 is not needed.
D. Add a step after step 5 to insert a SQL action that will use the values in the state record to populate the Program and Section fields of the Application Engine Call Section action.
E. Add a step after step 5 to select the Dynamic Call check box in the Call Section action.
F. Step 4 is wrong. The PeopleCode program should use the AESection class to issue the dynamic call.

Correct Answer: E

QUESTION 27

An Application Engine program requires a loop that will exit after 1000 rows have been processed. The COUNTER field in the state record is incremented in each iteration of the loop. Which option contains code that could be used in a Do While action to test for COUNTER?

A. Do While %Bind(Counter) < 1000
B. %SELECT (COUNTER) FROM PS_INSTALLATION Where COUNTER < 1000
C. If %Bind(Counter) >= 1000 then Exit;
D. %Select(COUNTER) FROM PS_STATE_AET Where COUNTER < 1000
E. %Select(COUNTER) SELECT 'X'
   FROM PS_INSTALLATION WHERE %Bind(COUNTER) < 1000;

Correct Answer: E

QUESTION 28

View the Exhibit.

As the developer, what do you need to do to make this PeopleSoft Application Engine program restartable?

A. Set the state record to derived/work.
B. Remove all section-level and step-level auto commits.
C. Nothing more. The Do Select action is set to Restartable.
D. Select the Disable Restart check box on the Program Properties page.
E. Deselect the Disable Restart check box on the Program Properties page.

Correct Answer: E

QUESTION 29

You use a PeopleCode program to build a dynamic SQL Select statement for an Application Engine program. Where would you place the PeopleCode program?
A. In a SQL action.
B. In a SQL definition.
C. In a PreBuild event.
D. In a Do While action.
E. In a Do Select action.
F. In a PeopleCode action

Correct Answer: F

QUESTION 30

View the Exhibit.

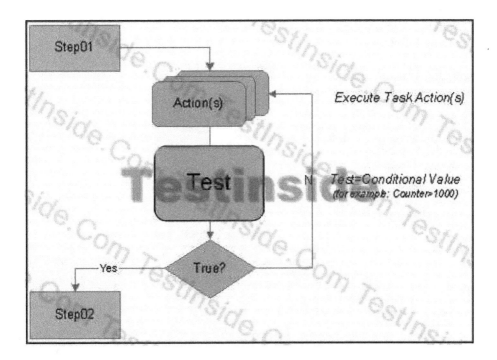

Which PeopleSoft Application Engine action is represented by the box labeled Test?

A. Do Select
B. Do While
C. Do Until
D. Do When
E. Do If
F. Do Loop

Correct Answer: C

QUESTION 31

What steps would you take to debug an Application Engine program using the PeopleSoft Application Engine debugger? (Choose all that apply.)

A. View the Debug log in Process Monitor.
B. View the results in the Debugger window.
C. View the file DBG1.tmp in the Temp directory.

D. Execute the Application Engine program from Application Designer.
E. In Application Designer, select Debug, Application Engine Debug Mode.
F. Select the Debug check box on the Process Scheduler tab in Configuration Manager.
G. On the sign-on page, select the debug settings for PeopleSoft Application Engine Debug.

Correct Answer: BDF

QUESTION 32

View the Exhibit.

```
File  Edit  Format  Help
-- PeopleTools 8.48 -- Application Engine
-- Copyright (c) 1988, 2007, Oracle.
-- All rights reserved.
-- Database: T1B84801 (SqlServer)

                        PeopleSoft Application Engine Timings
                             (All timings in seconds)
                           2007-06-12  20.43.26

                            C o m p i l e     E x e c u t e     F e t c h         Total
SQL Statement               Count    Time     Count    Time     Count   Time      Time
------------------------     -------  -------- -------- -------- ------- --------  --------

PeopleCode

SELECT PS_PERF_TUN_AET                          500     19.1     500    2.3       21.4
SELECT PS_PERF_TUN_AET or Your Label Here       500      8.3       0    0.0        8.3
                                                                                 --------
                                                                                  29.7

Application Engine

CHKPOINT                    0        0.0      1004     74.2       0      0.0       74.2
COMMIT                      0        0.0      1004      4.4       0      0.0        4.4
LOGMSG                      0        0.0         1      0.1       0      0.0        0.1
                                                                                 --------
                                                                                  78.7

AE Program: PERF_TUN

MAIN.Delete.S               1        0.0         1      0.0       0      0.0        0.0
MAIN.GetTEXT.S              1        0.0         1      0.0       1      0.0        0.0
MAIN.PCodLoop.W             501      3.7       501      3.8       501    0.0        7.4
                                                                                 --------
                                                                                   7.5
```

Note the values in the CHKPOINT row.

This program is taking much longer to run than it needs to.

The ability to restart without compromising data integrity is crucial. The program has the Disable Restart check box deselected.
What is one area of opportunity to cut processing time?

A. Reduce the frequency of commits.
B. Reduce the number of checkpoints by using Bulk Insert.
C. Replace section-level or step-level auto commits with explicit commits within SQL steps.

D. Use a derived/work record for the state record so that checkpoints are stored in memory instead of in a SQL table.

E. PeopleCode records checkpoints much more quickly than SQL actions, so execute SQL using PeopleCode actions wherever possible.

Correct Answer: A

QUESTION 33

View the Exhibit.

The following table describes the available TRACE option parameter values:

Value	Description
0	Disables tracing.
1	Initiates the Application Engine step trace.
2	Initiates the Application Engine SQL trace.
4	Initiates the trace for dedicated temporary table allocation to an Application Engine trace (AET) file. You can trace how the system allocates, locks, and releases temporary tables during program runs.
128	Initiates the statement timings trace to a file, which is similar to the COBOL timings trace to a file.
256	Initiates the PeopleCode detail to the file for the timings trace.
1024	Initiates the statement timings trace, but stores the results in the following tables: PS_BAT_TIMINGS_LOG and PS_BAT_TIMINGS_DTL.
2048	Requests a database optimizer trace file.
4096	Requests a database optimizer to be inserted in the Explain Plan table of the current database.
8192	Sets a trace for PeopleSoft Integration Broker transform programs.

You want to add trace parameters to an Application Engine command line. Which trace parameters will trace steps, SQL, and PeopleCode?

A. TRACE 1 2 256
B. TRACE 1,2,256
C. TRACE (1,2,256)

D. TRACE 1 -TRACE 2 -TRACE 256

E. TRACE 259

F. TRACE 512

G. TRACE 12256

Correct Answer: E

QUESTION 34

Set processing can improve Application Engine performance in many cases by_____.

A. caching selected rows in memory

B. using SQL to process groups of rows at one time

C. transferring SQL processing from the client to the application server

D. applying sophisticated data normalization algorithms based on set theory

E. using precompiled SQL in Application Engine libraries, rather than letting Application Engine parse each statement

Correct Answer: B

QUESTION 35

You add a button to a page to run an Application Engine program in synchronous mode. How do you configure the button?

A. Associate the button with a run control record that passes parameters to Process Scheduler to schedule the process.

B. Associate the button with FieldChange PeopleCode that uses a Process Request object to schedule the process.

C. Associate the button with FieldChange PeopleCode that uses a CallAppEngine function to launch the program.

D. Associate the button with an Application Engine PeopleCode action that passes parameters to a Call Section action.

E. Associate the button with OnExecute PeopleCode that uses a PSAE command to launch the program.

Correct Answer: C

QUESTION 36

View the Exhibit.

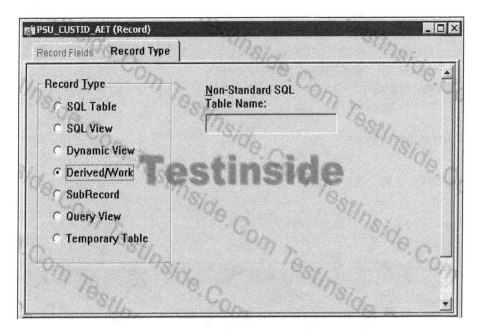

This is the state record for the PSU_CUST_CHG Application Engine program.

How will selecting a Record Type of Derived/Work for the state record affect the program PSU_CUST_CHG at run time?

A. It will execute as expected only if it does not update database tables.
B. It will execute as expected unless the program needs to be restarted.
C. It will execute, but performance could be improved by using SQL View.
D. It will abend (abnormal end) because the Record Type for a state record must be SQL Table.
E. It will abend (abnormal end) because the Record Type for a state record must be Temporary Table.

Correct Answer: B

QUESTION 37

Select two uses of the Program Flow view in PeopleSoft Application Engine Designer. (Choose two.)

A. Testing SQL statements
B. Ordering the steps in a program
C. Checking the syntax of PeopleCode
D. Viewing the expected sequence of steps
E. Viewing program flow during execution
F. Launching editors for SQL and PeopleCode

Correct Answer: DF

QUESTION 38

View the Exhibit.

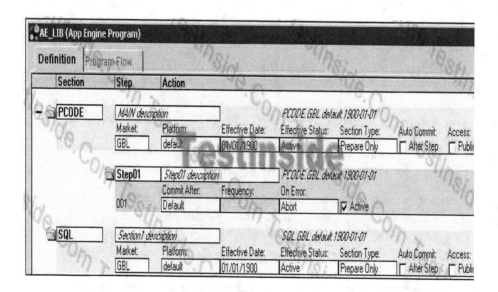

You want to reuse the code in this Application Engine program by making it available to other Application Engine programs.

What must you do to use the program as a repository for PeopleSoft Application Engine sections?

A. Delete the MAIN section.
B. Rename the MAIN section.
C. Use the suffix LIB in the program name.
D. Include at least one Call Section action.
E. Set Access to Public for at least one section.
F. Select the Application Library check box on the Advanced tabbed page of the PeopleSoft Application Engine Properties dialog.

Correct Answer: E

QUESTION 39

View the Exhibit.

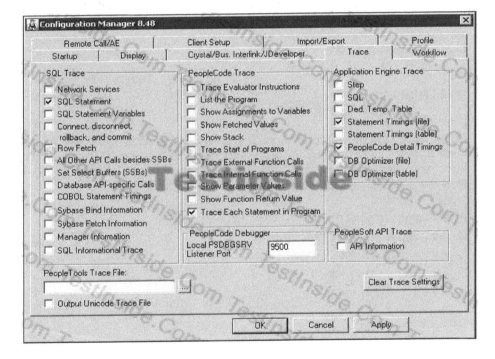

You run an Application Engine program through Process Scheduler with Trace configured as shown in the Exhibit.
What will the trace show? (Choose all that apply.)

A. SQL statements
B. Statement Timings
C. PeopleCode Detail Timings
D. Trace Each Statement in Program
E. Nothing. The program has to be run in two-tier mode.
F. Nothing. A PeopleTools Trace File must be specified.

Correct Answer: E

QUESTION 40

An Application Engine program incorporates PeopleCode and SQL. Which three statements are correct? (Choose three.)

A. All SQL statements are executed using SQL actions.
B. All PeopleCode is executed using PeopleCode actions.
C. SQL Select statements can be used to control program flow.
D. Steps are the smallest unit of work that can be committed within a program.
E. If a program executes a step with a SQL Insert or Update statement, it must also execute a step with a Commit action before completion.

Correct Answer: BCD

QUESTION 41

An Application Engine program section uses a SQL Select statement to select fields from the CUST_ORDERS table, and then calls a section that uses a SQL Insert statement to update the CUST_HISTORY table based on those fields. How are the field values passed between the SQL statements?

A. By using state variables
B. By using a state record
C. By using a SQL view
D. By using meta variables
E. By using a SQL cursor

Correct Answer: B

QUESTION 42
An Application Engine program has a SQL action with the following code:
INSERT INTO %Table(AETEST_TAO)
(PROCESS_INSTANCE

, AE_INT_1

, AE_APPLID

, AE_SECTION)

SELECT %ProcessInstance

, %Bind (AE_INT_1)

, %AEProgram
, %AESection

FROM PS_INSTALLATION

What is the purpose of the %Table construct?

A. %Table resolves to the correct state record.
B. %Table can improve performance by caching the table in memory.
C. %Table resolves to the assigned temporary table instance at run time.
D. %Table populates the state record with the results of the Select statement.

Correct Answer: C

QUESTION 43

On the Service Operation definition page, the Introspection link is used to_____

A. provide a Web service
B. consume a Web service
C. add a new service operation
D. add a new service operation version
E. add routing to existing service operation

Correct Answer: E

QUESTION 44

Which two modifications can you make to an individual component interface property? (Choose two.)

A. Change the name.
B. Set up synchronization.
C. Add a user-defined method.
D. Expose a standard method.
E. Make the property read-only.

Correct Answer: AE

QUESTION 45

You can use the ExecuteEdits method in handler code to_____.

A. call a component interface
B. invoke the standard system edits
C. execute a PeopleCode built-in function
D. call PeopleCode validation built-in functions
E. call an application engine program from the receiving process

Correct Answer: B

QUESTION 46

View the Exhibit, which shows the file layout for SETID_FILE.

You have been asked to write the PeopleCode to export SETIDs to a flat file, along with an action row indicating whether the action is an addition or a change.

The resulting flat file will contain a row indicating the action followed by a row containing transaction data. The PeopleCode will be placed on the SETID_TBL.SETID.SavePostChange event.

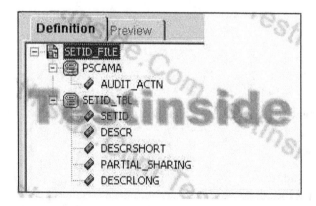

Which set of statements will write both the AUDIT_ACTN and SETID_TBL rows to the file?

A. &SETID = SETID_TBL.SETID;
   If %Mode = "A" Then &rRec1.AUDIT_ACTN.Value = "A";
   Else
   &rRec1.AUDIT_ACTN.Value = "C"; End-If;

```
&SETIDOUT.WriteRecord(&rRec1); &rRec2 = GetRecord();
&SETIDOUT.WriteRowset(&rRec2);
```

B.
```
&SETID = SETID_TBL.SETID;
If %Mode = "A" Then &rRec1.AUDIT_ACTN.Value = "A";
Else
&rRec1.AUDIT_ACTN.Value = "C"; End-If;
&SETIDOUT.WriteRecord(&rRec1); &rRec2 = GetRecord();
&SETIDOUT.WriteRecord(&rRec2);
```
C.
```
&SETID = SETID_TBL.SETID;
If %Mode = "A" Then &rRec1.AUDIT_ACTN.Value = "A";
Else &rRec1.AUDIT_ACTN.Value = "C"; End-If;

&SETIDOUT.WriteRowset(&rRec1); &rRec2 = GetRecord();
&SETIDOUT.WriteRowset(&rRec2);
```

Correct Answer: B

QUESTION 47

You have been asked to configure the Integration Gateway on your local Web server. You entered the Gateway

URL, loaded the connectors, and successfully pinged the Gateway. You select the Domain Status page to activate your domain, however, you cannot find your domain listed. To activate the domain, you need to_____

A. reboot the Web server
B. purge the domain status
C. purge the application server cache
D. start Pub/Sub on the application server
E. use the Integration Broker Quick Configuration page

Correct Answer: D

QUESTION 48

Component interface Find keys are mapped to_____.

A. all keys in a component search record
B. search keys in a component search record
C. duplicate order keys in a component search record
D. alternate search key in a component search record

E. search and alternate search keys in a component

Correct Answer: E

QUESTION 49

Which type of message is most often used for PeopleSoft-to-PeopleSoft integrations?

A. Rowset-based message
B. Rowset-based message parts
C. Non-rowset-based message
D. Non-rowset-based message parts

Correct Answer: A

QUESTION 50

View the Exhibit that shows the PeopleCode to publish the CUSTOMER service operation.

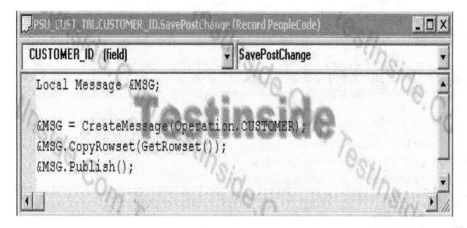

This code has been placed in the SavePostChange event in the CUSTOMER_ID field in the PSU_CUST_TBL record. When a user updates the customer in the PeopleSoft Pure Internet Architecture and saves the page, what data from the page will be copied into the message structure?

A. The entire rowset
B. Only the rows of data at level0
C. Only the rows of data at level 1
D. Only the rows of data that have changed in the rowset
E. The original values of the changed rows, as well as the rows of data that

have changed

Correct Answer: A

QUESTION 51

Which two characteristics are required to create Transform type application engine programs? (Choose two).

A. The Program Type is Transform Only.
B. The Action Type is either XSLT or PeopleCode.
C. You must set the Graphical Mapper option to Yes.
D. You must define the psft_function in the application engine program.
E. The input and output message names must be defined in the application engine program properties, even if Oracle Graphical Mapper is not used.

Correct Answer: AB

QUESTION 52

Which three URLs must be defined before you can create messages and schemas? (Choose three.)

A. Inquiry URL
B. Publish URL
C. Target location
D. Service namespace
E. Schema namespace

Correct Answer: CDE

QUESTION 53

You created a component interface and now must implement it on an online component. The PeopleCode that triggers a component interface is placed on the SavePostChange event. Select the three reasons for placing the PeopleCode on the SavePostChange event? (Choose three.)

A. SavePostChange event is not field dependent.
B. SavePostChange is initiated after the Component Processor updates the database.
C. SavePostChange is generally used to update tables that are not in the component.
D. An error or warning that is generated in SavePostChange causes the component interface to be canceled, but the component data is saved.

E. The system issues a SQL commit after the SavePostChange terminates successfully.

Correct Answer: BCE

QUESTION 54

Select three characteristics of the Default User ID field that you define for a node. (Choose three.)

A. It is required for all nodes.
B. It is used for inbound service operations.
C. It is used for outbound service operations.
D. You specify a value for the field only when you set the authentication option to None.
E. It is used when a third party invokes a service operation without an authentication user ID and password.

Correct Answer: ABE

QUESTION 55

Published services are stored in the PeopleSoft database in the_____table.

A. PSIBWSDL
B. PSIBPROFILE
C. PSIBUDDI_VW
D. PSIBRTNGDEFN
E. PSIBUDDISETUP
F. PSIBMSGSCHEMA

Correct Answer: A

QUESTION 56

Logical transformations are required to_____.

A. send or receive a nonrowset-based message
B. alias the current version of the service operation
C. send or receive a service operation using an alias
D. send or receive nondefault versions of a service operation
E. change the message for the current version of the service operation

Correct Answer: D

QUESTION 57

You created a component interface with the standard methods of Create, Find, Get, Cancel, and Save. You secured the component interface and provided full access to all the methods. You want to test the GET method to access the online information. Which three steps will you use to test the GET method? (Choose three.)

A. Open the component interface in Application Designer.
B. Right-click in the component interface view and select Test Component Interface.
C. Save the data by selecting File, Save.
D. Use the Find option to test the GET method after supplying key values.
E. Use the Get Existing option to test the GET method after supplying key values.
F. Enter data in the Component Interface Tester tool.
G. Validate that the data has been modified and saved by accessing the online component or using the database query tool.

Correct Answer: ABE

QUESTION 58

You created a component interface and now must implement it on an online component. The PeopleCode must instantiate the component interface. Which five steps are needed to instantiate the component interface? (Choose five)

A. Establish a session with the %Session system variable.
B. Establish a session with the Connect method.
C. Use the GetComplntfc method.
D. Set key values.
E. If the key uniquely defines a component interface, then execute the Find method.
F. Get or set property values.
G. Run the Cancel method and then the Save method.
H. Run the Save method.

Correct Answer : ACDFH

QUESTION 59

View the Exhibit that shows the message tree structure for the STUDENT_INFO message.

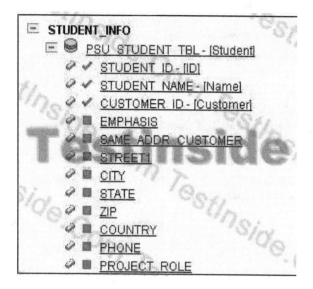

Based on this structure, which two statements describe the message? (Choose two.)

A. This is a rowset-based message.
B. Student is an alias for the record.
C. This is a non-rowset-based message.
D. The alias for this message is Student.
E. The description for the STUDENT_ID field is ID.
F. The EMPHASIS field is included in the message.

Correct Answer: AB

QUESTION 60

Which two tasks do you need to complete after consuming a Web service? (Choose two.)

A. Add a point-to-point routing.
B. Add the appropriate OnRequest handler.
C. Secure the service operation with a permission list.
D. Write the PeopleCode to invoke the service operation.
E. Update the connection properties on the service operation.

Correct Answer: CD

QUESTION 61

Select three components of the integration gateway. (Choose three.)

A. XML Parsing
B. Target connectors
C. Listening connectors
D. Performance throttling
E. Transformation engine
F. Data handling dispatchers and handlers

Correct Answer: ABC

QUESTION 62

You created a component interface based on a component that has a parent PSU_STUDENT_TBL and one non-effective-dated child record PSU_STUDENT_EXP.

The component interface PeopleCode was created by a developer and a snippet of that PeopleCode is as follows:

```
&oPsuStudentExpCollection = &oStuProfile2.PSU_STUDENT_EXP; &item =
&oPsuStudentExpCollection.ItemByKeys("PT");
If &item <> Null Then

&j = &item.ItemNum;

&oPsuStudentExp = &oPsuStudentExpCollection.Item(&j);

If &oPsuStudentExp.SKILL = "PT" And &oPsuStudentExp.PROFICIENCY = "L"

Then

&oPsuStudentExp.PROFICIENCY = "M"; End-If;
```

Else

```
&oPsuStudentExp = &oPsuStudentExpCollection.InsertItem(1);
&oPsuStudentExp.SKILL = "PT"; &oPsuStudentExp.PROFICIENCY = "M";
&oPsuStudentExp.DATE_LAST_MAINT = PSU_CRS_SESSN.END_DATE;
```

End-If;
Which statement best describes what this snippet of PeopleCode is trying to accomplish?

A. Inserts a child row and sets the SKILL, PROFICIENCY, and DATE_LAST_MAINT values, if SKILL is not equal to T

B. Insert a child row and sets the SKILL, PROFICIENCY, and DATE_LAST_MAINT values, if SKILL is equal to T

C. Inserts a child row and sets the SKILL, PROFICIENCY and DATE_LAST_MAINT values, if SKILL is equal to "PT" and PROFICENCY is equal to

D. Modifies the PROFICIENCY of a child row if SKILL is T and PROFICIENCY is for that row

E. Modifies the value of PROFICIENCY of the child row in which SKILL is T and PROFCIENCY is , else if SKILL is not T inserts a child row and sets the SKILL, PROFICIENCY, and DATE_LAST_MAINT value

Correct Answer: E

QUESTION 63

You are asked to create a new service operation that will enable a third-party system to inquire on an item price and receive the response in real time. Which operation type would you use when you create the service operation?

A. Synchronous
B. Asynchronous one-way
C. Asynchronous-to-synchronous
D. Asynchronous request/response

Correct Answer: A

QUESTION 64

You have been asked to create the handler for an asynchronous service operation that is being sent outbound to several external nodes. When the service operation is sent, you need to be able to add criteria to filter the nodes. Which method will you implement in the handler PeopleCode to accomplish this?
A. OnNotify

B. OnRouteSend

C. OnAckReceive

D. OnRequestSend

E. OnRouteReceive

Correct Answer: B Section: (none) Explanation

QUESTION 65

You have recently installed PeopleSoft HCM system. To populate employee information into the PERSONS table from your legacy system, you will read in a CSV flat file.
Which are the four steps you need to create the file layout on the HCM system to import the data? (Choose four.)

A. Provide the import data in a correctly formatted flat file.

B. Write the Application Engine program to export the data.

C. Preview and troubleshoot the input data format and content.

D. Set the File Record ID on the File Layout segment properties.

E. Set the file layout properties to specify the file layout format of CSV.

F. Create a file layout to match the record and field structure of the data.

Correct Answer: ACEF

QUESTION 66

Which IntBroker class method do you use to send a synchronous request?

A. Publish

B. InboundPublish

C. SyncRequest

D. GetSyncIBInfoData

E. ConnectorRequest

Correct Answer: C

QUESTION 67

You have been asked to import a CSV file. You create the file layout definition for the record structure and enter your default file name on the Preview tab. When you preview the file, only the first column of the preview grid is populated. What will you do to correct this problem?

A. change the file layout format to match the input file

B. specify file record IDs that match the input file records

C. increase the field length to accommodate the input data

D. change the definition delimiter to match the one that is used in the input file

E. decrease the start position and adjust the field length to match the input data start position and length

Correct Answer: D

QUESTION 68

When you created a new component interface, you selected "Accept Default Values". Which two things are automatically added to the component interface? (Choose two.)

A. Keys are created based on the component search record.

B. No fields or records are added to the component interface view.

C. Only Find keys and Get keys are created for the component interface.

D. All primary fields and records are exposed in the component interface.

E. Only Create keys and Get keys are created for the component interface.

Correct Answer: AD

QUESTION 69

When you service-enable a component interface, the request message shape for the Get method contains_____.

A. Get keys

B. Find keys

C. Object key

D. CI buffer structure

E. Find key collection

Correct Answer: A

QUESTION 70

View the Exhibit that shows the PeopleCode used to publish the LOCATION_SYNC service operation.

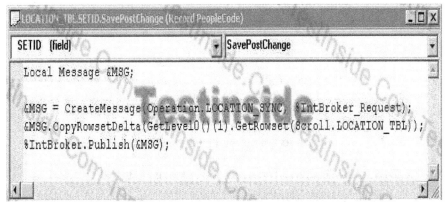

```
LOCATION_TBL.SETID.SavePostChange (Record PeopleCode)                    _ □ X

SETID (field)                              ▼  SavePostChange              ▼

  Local Message &MSG;

  &MSG = CreateMessage(Operation.LOCATION_SYNC, &IntBroker_Request);
  &MSG.CopyRowsetDelta(GetLevel0()(1).GetRowset(Scroll.LOCATION_TBL));
  &IntBroker.Publish(&MSG);

◄                                                                          ►
```

This code has been placed in the SavePostChange event in the SETID field in the LOCATION_TBL record. When a user updates the location in the PeopleSoft Pure Internet Architecture and saves the page, what data from the page will be copied into the message structure?

A. The entire rowset
B. Only the rows of data at level 0
C. Only the rows of data at level 1
D. Only the rows of data that have changed in the rowset
E. The original values of the changed rows, as well as the rows of data that have changed

Correct Answer: D

QUESTION 71

Which statement describes a container message?

A. The container can be nested.
B. The resulting shape is always rowset based.
C. PSCAMA is automatically added to the schema.
D. The resulting shape is always nonrowset based.
E. The message parts can be a mixture of rowset based and nonrowset based.

Correct Answer: D

QUESTION 72

You are expecting a flat file from a third-party system. The file contains information to populate a table on your HCM system. But the data being supplied will contain only a few of the record fields in the PERSON table defined in your HCM system. Further, the file has a control file field that will indicate whether to add, change, or update the information.

The file format is:

999 A /* Indicates the action to take */001 1000 Smith,John 123 Easy Street Easy City CA /*Actual Data*/ 999 C 001 1020 Jones, Tom 1024 Hard Life Street Hardknocks NJ

Which are the two choices to define the file layout? (Choose two.)

A. The file layout will contain two segments. One using the record field PSCAMA.AUDIT_ACTN and the other the record fields from PERSON - EMPLID, NAME, STREET, CITY, and STATE.
B. The file layout will contain one segment for PSCAMA.AUDIT_ACTN and one child segment for PERSON.
C. The File Record ID in the File Layout Segment Properties for the PSCAMA segment will be 001.
D. The File Record ID in the File Layout Segment Properties for the PSCAMA segment will be 999 and for PERSON 001.
E. The File Record ID in the File Layout Segment Properties for the PSCAMA segment will be 999 and no File Record ID is needed for PERSON.

Correct Answer: AD

QUESTION 73

You created a component interface based on a component that has a parent PSU_CRS_SESSN and one non-effective-dated child record PSU_STU_ENROLL.

The component interface PeopleCode was created by a developer and a snippet of that PeopleCode is as follows:

&oPsuStuEnrollCollection = &oPsuCrsEnroll.PSU_STU_ENROLL;

For &i = 1 To &oPsuStuEnrollCollection.Count &oPsuStuEnroll = &oPsuStuEnrollCollection.Item(&i);

If &oPsuStuEnroll.ENROLL_STATUS = "ENR" then
&oPsuStuEnroll.ENROLL_STATUS = "RES";
End-if End-For;

Which statement best describes what this snippet of PeopleCode is trying to accomplish?

A. Inserts a child row if ENROLL_STATUS = ENR

B. Modifies each child row in which ENROLL_STATUS =ENR

C. Inserts a child row if any row has ENROLL_STATUS = ENR

D. Modifies each child row if any row has ENROLL_STATUS = ENR

Correct Answer: B

QUESTION 74

View the Exhibit that shows the definition for the PO_QUEUE queue

Which three statements describe how this queue will function? (Choose three.)

A. Messages will be processed in parallel.

B. All messages will be processed sequentially in the order in which they are sent.

C. If an error occurs on a message, all subsequent messages will remain in a status of New.

D. If an error occurs on a message, all messages except those with the same high-level key will continue to process.

E. When the PeopleSoft Integration Broker archive process is run, the system will delete message transaction data from the current run-time tables.

F. When the PeopleSoft Integration Broker archive process is run, the system will write message transaction data to the archive tables and delete the data from the current run-time tables.

Correct Answer: BCF

QUESTION 75

You are testing a new asynchronous service operation to send employee job data to another system; however, no operation instance is created. Select three possible causes. (Choose three.)
A. The sending node is paused.
B. The sending domain is not active.
C. No Publication PeopleCode exists.
D. Publication PeopleCode is incorrect.
E. No outbound routings exist for the service operation.
F. The service operation is not active on the receiving system.

Correct Answer: CDE

QUESTION 76

The Application Engine program PSU_PROC_CRSE has a Do Select action with the following code:

%Select (COURSE, EFFDT, DESCR, TOOLS_REL) SELECT COURSE
, EFFDT

, DESCR

, TOOLS_REL

FROM PS_PSU_COURSE_TBL A

WHERE A.EFFDT <= (SELECT MAX(A1.EFFDT) FROM PS_PSU_COURSE_TBL A1
WHERE A1.COURSE = A.COURSe AND A1.EFFDT <= GETDATE())
The program works fine in testing, but it fails when run on an Oracle database platform.

Select the two approaches that will resolve the problem and give the expected results. (Choose two.)

A. Delete the Where clause.
B. Change the WHERE clause to WHERE A.EFFDT = MAX(EFFDT).

C. Change the SELECT clause to SELECT DISTINCT.
D. Change the WHERE clause to WHERE %EffdtCheck(PSU_COURSE_TBL A, %CurrentDateIn).
E. Replace the GETDATE() function with the %CurrentDateIn system variable.
F. Select the Active check box on the step so that the PeopleSoft Application Engine automatically selects the current row.

Correct Answer: DE

QUESTION 77

An Application Engine program is structured with sections, steps, and actions. Which two statements are correct? (Choose two.)
A. Steps can call other steps.
B. Sections execute sequentially.
C. Steps can call other programs.
D. Steps execute alphabetically within a program.
E. Sections are ordered alphabetically following MAIN.

Correct Answer: CE

QUESTION 78

An Application Engine program includes a step that selects all the rows in the PS_ORDERS table where CUSTOMER_TYPE = PARTNER, and then calls a PeopleCode program that processes each row of data. Which should be the first action type in the step?

A. Do Select
B. Do When
C. Do While
D. Do Until
E. Do If
F. Do Query

Correct Answer: A

QUESTION 79

What is required in order to use an Application Engine Call Section action to call a portion of another Application Engine program?

A. The called step is set to Public.
B. The called action is set to Public.

C. The Call Section action must specify the program name and section.
D. The Call Section action must specify the program name, section, and step.
E. The called program has Application Library selected in the program properties.
F. A Call Section action can never call a portion of another Application Engine program.

Correct Answer: C

QUESTION 80

View the Exhibit.

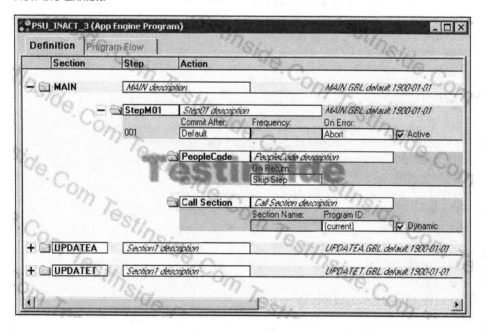

The PeopleCode action contains this code: If AE_STATEREC_AET.TYPE =
Then
 AE_STATEREC_AET.AE_SECTION= PDATEA
 Else

 AE_STATEREC_AET.AE_SECTION= PDATET

 End-If;

What will be the result?

A. The Call Section will call either UPDATEA or UPDATET based on the value of AE_STATEREC_AET.TYPE.
B. The Call Section action will show an error. The PeopleCode program also needs to populate the field AE_STATEREC_AET.AE_APPLID.
C. The Call Section action will show an error. The PeopleCode program also needs to populate the field AE_STATEREC_AET.AE_APPLID, not AE_STATEREC_AET.AE_SECTION.
D. The Call Section action will not execute because the PeopleCode program needs to pass values to the state record using bind variables.
E. The Call Section action will show an error because UPDATEA and UPDATET are not public sections.

Correct Answer: A

QUESTION 81

The Application Engine program PSU_PROC_ORD uses values from PS_PSU_ORDER_DTL and PS_PSU_STOCK_TBL to update PS_PSU_STOCK_TBL. You used a Do Select action to select QTY_ON_HAND, QTY_ORDERED, and ITEM_CD from PS_PSU_ORDER_DTL into the state record. You added a SQL action to update PS_PSU_STOCK_TBL using the values in the state record. Which code would you use in the SQL action?

A. UPDATE PS_PSU_STOCK_TBL SET QTY_ON_HAND = %1 - %2 WHERE ITEM_CD = %3
(QTY_ON_HAND, QTY_ORDERED, ITEM_CD)
B. %UPDATE (QTY_ON_HAND)
SELECT QTY_ON_HAND - QTY_ORDERED FROM PS_PSU_STOCK_TBL WHERE ITEM_CD = %Bind(ITEM_CD)
C. UPDATE PS_PSU_STOCK_TBL
SET QTY_ON_HAND = %Bind(QTY_ON_HAND) - %Bind(QTY_ORDERED) WHERE ITEM_CD = %Bind(ITEM_CD)
D. UPDATE PS_PSU_STOCK_TBL
SET QTY_ON_HAND = Bind(QTY_ON_HAND) - Bind(QTY_ORDERED) WHERE ITEM_CD = Bind(ITEM_CD)
E. %UPDATE PS_PSU_STOCK_TBL
SET QTY_ON_HAND = %QTY_ON_HAND - %QTY_ORDERED) WHERE ITEM_CD = %ITEM_CD

Correct Answer: C

QUESTION 82

Which component is used to associate a code set group with a node?

A. Nodes
B. Codesets
C. Messages
D. Codeset Value
E. Codeset Groups
F. Service Operations

Correct Answer: A

QUESTION 83

View the Exhibit.

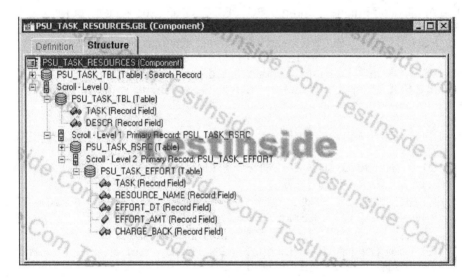

This PeopleCode program disables the CHARGE_BACK field: Local Row
&Row;
&Row = GetRow(); &Row.PSU_TASK_EFFORT.CHARGE_BACK.Enabled =
False;
For this program to work as shown, what is the highest level at which it could be
placed?

A. PSU_TASK_TBL (Table)
B. PSU_TASK_RSRC (Table)
C. PSU_TASK_EFFORT (Table)
D. CHARGE_BACK (Record Field)

E. PSU_TASK_RESOURCES (Component)

F. PSU_TASK_TBL (Table) - Search Record

Correct Answer: C

QUESTION 84

Your customer presents you with a requirement for an Application Engine program that performs massive updates to reporting tables based on each day transactions. The requirements are:

The Application Engine program must complete all processing within a four-hour window.

In the event of an abend, there must be a way for the program to resume processing where it stopped. What are your three design considerations? (Choose three.)

A. Using a state record with a type of derived/work will improve processing speed, but field values will be lost if there is an abend.

B. Using a run control record with a type of derived/work will improve processing speed, but field values will be lost if there is an abend.

C. If the program commits frequently, less work will be lost if a restart is needed. However, each commit takes processing time.

D. If the program commits frequently, fewer benchmarks are needed, which saves time. However, more work must be redone if a restart is needed.

E. If the Disable Restart checkbox is selected for an Application program, processing time is reduced because Application Engine does not record checkpoints. However, the developer must build restart logic into the program.

F. If the Disable Restart check box is not selected, derived/work state record field values are stored to PS_AERUNCONTROL before each commit. However, using a derived/work state record improves processing speed.

Correct Answer: ACE

QUESTION 85

You are receiving a FIXED formatted file from an outside vendor. You want to import the file data into your PeopleSoft system. However, the description field on the file has commas inserted and you want to eliminate them before populating your system tables. Which are the five steps you need to perform to create the file layout on your system to import the data and eliminate the extraneous characters in a field? (Choose five.)

A. Write the application engine program to export the data.
B. Provide the import data in a correctly formatted flat file.
C. Create a file layout to match the record and field structure of the data.
D. Set the file layout properties to specify the file layout format of FIXED.
E. On the Preview tab, enter a comma as the strip character on the description field.
F. Set the File Record ID on the File Layout segment properties.
G. Preview and troubleshoot the input data format and content.
H. On the Preview tab, enter a comma as the field qualifier on the description field.

Correct Answer: BCDEG

QUESTION 86

View the Exhibit.

```
-- PeopleTools 8.48 -- Application Engine
--- Copyright (c) 1988, 2006, oracle.
-- All rights reserved.
-- Database: T1B84801 (SqlServer)


                    PeopleSoft Application Engine Timings
                           (All timings in seconds)
                           2006-06-19  14.20.33

                        C o m p i l e    E x e c u t e    F e t c h        Total
SQL Statement           Count    Time    Count    Time    Count   Time     Time


Peoplecode

SELECT PS_PERF_TUN_AET                     500     12.9     500     1.9    14.8
SELECT PS_PERF_TUN_AET or Your Label Here  500      5.6       0     0.0     5.6
                                                                          -------
                                                                           20.4

Application Engine

CHKPOINT                   0     0.0    1004     54.6      0      0.0     54.6
COMMIT                     0     0.0    1004      3.5      0      0.0      3.5
LOGMSG                     0     0.0       1      0.0      0      0.0      0.0
                                                                        -------
                                                                         58.1

AE Program: PERF_TUN

MAIN.Delete.S              1     0.0       1      0.0      0      0.0      0.0
MAIN.GetTEXT.S             1     0.0       1      0.0      1      0.0      0.0
MAIN.Loop.W              501     2.6     501      4.1    501      0.0      6.8
                                                                        -------
                                                                          6.8


                        Call    Non-SQL   SQL    Total
Peoplecode              Count    Time     Time    Time

AE Program: PERF_TUN

PCODLOOP.INSERT           500     22.6     20.4    43.0
PCODLOOP.PCcnt+1          500      3.6      0.0     3.6
                                -------  ------  -------
                                  26.1     20.4    46.6
```

Note the Application Engine action MAIN.Loop.W

Setting the Action Type to ReUse can significantly reduce the run time for certain Application Engine programs. Is this program a good candidate for ReUse, and why?

A. Yes. ReUse is most effective in a SQL looping construct.
B. Yes. ReUse reduces compile time for PeopleCode statements.
C. No. ReUse reduces compile time for PeopleCode, but this loop is in a Do While action.
D. No. ReUse is most effective in a SQL looping construct, but this loop is in a PeopleCode action.
E. Yes. ReUse reduces the number of checkpoints because fewer SQL Insert statements are performed.

Correct Answer: A

QUESTION 87

An Application Engine program has a Do While action with the following code:

%SELECT (TEMP_FLD) SELECT 'COUNTER' FROM PS_INSTALLATION WHERE %Bind(COUNTER) < 1000;

What will be the result?

A. The program will abend because PS_INSTALLATION does not have a COUNTER field.
B. The Do While action will go into an infinite loop because the Select statement will always return true.
C. The actions following the Do While action will never execute because the Select will never return true.
D. The Do While will execute at least once, no matter what the result of the Select.
E. The Do While will execute as expected, as long as COUNTER is being incremented in PS_INSTALLATION for every loop.
F. The Do While will execute as expected, as long as COUNTER is being incremented in the state record for every loop.

Correct Answer: F

QUESTION 88

When you service-enable a component interface, the response message shape for the Get method contains_____.

A. Get keys
B. Find keys
C. Object key
D. CI buffer structure
E. Find key collection

Correct Answer: D

QUESTION 89

You have recently installed PeopleSoft HCM system. To populate employee information into the PERSON, ADDRESSES, and NAMES tables, you will read in an XML flat file from a non-PeopleSoft system.
PERSON is the parent table and ADDRESSES and NAMES are the child tables of PERSON.

Which two steps will you need to perform to create the file layout on the HCM system? (Choose two.)

A. Write the application engine program to export the data.
B. Provide the import data in a correctly formatted flat file.
C. Create a file layout to match the record and field structure of the data.
D. Set the file layout properties to specify the file layout format of XML.
E. Preview and troubleshoot the input data format and content.
F. Enter file record IDs on the file layout segment properties.
G. Adjust the start position of all file fields after the start position of the file record.

Correct Answer: CD

QUESTION 90

Select a good reason to select Disable Restart in an Application Engine program.
A. The program commits every row.
B. Selecting Disable Restart improves performance because it causes Application Engine to defer all commits until processing completes.
C. The program does a lot of preparation work up front, like joining tables and loading data into temporary work tables.
D. The program only commits once, when the program successfully completes.
E. The program performs crucial and time-sensitive data processing.

Correct Answer: D

QUESTION 91

You created a component interface based on a component that has a parent and one non-effective-dated child (Level 0 and 1). You have been asked to write the PeopleCode to insert a new row in the collection if the row does not exist. In order to determine whether the row already exists, which method will you use?

A. InsertItem()
B. ItembyKeys()
C. CurrentItem()
D. GetEffectiveItem()
E. GetEffectiveItemNum()

Correct Answer: B

QUESTION 92

You have been asked to create an application class to consume the asynchronous service operation ADD_COURSE. The requirements state that you should execute all the standard edits for COURSE_TBL and throw an exception if an error occurs. Complete the second line in this code: If &msg.IsEditError Then _____

Exit (1);

A. %IntBroker.SetStatus(&msg,%Operation_New)
B. %IntBroker.SetStatus(&msg,%Operation_Canceled)
C. %IntBroker.SetStatus(&msg,%Operation_Error)
D. &MyErrors = %IntBroker.GetMessageErrors(&TransactionId);

Correct Answer: C

QUESTION 93

Examine this PeopleCode snippet:

&SQL = CreateSQL("Select %EffDtCheck(EFFDT) from %Table(PSU_INSTR_TBL)"); Select the correct option.

A. The statement is valid.
B. The statement is not valid. The correct syntax is:
&SQL = CreateSQL("Select %DateIn(EFFDT) from %Table(PSU_INSTR_TBL)");
C. The statement is not valid. The correct syntax is:

```
&SQL = CreateSQL("Select %DateOut(EFFDT) from
%Table(PSU_INSTR_TBL)");
```

D. The statement is not valid. The correct syntax is:
```
&SQL = CreateSQL("Select %CurrDate(EFFDT) from
%Table(PSU_INSTR_TBL)");
```

E. The statement is not valid. The correct syntax is:
```
&SQL = CreateSQL("Select %Date(EFFDT) from
%Table(PSU_INSTR_TBL)");
```

F. The statement is not valid. The correct syntax is:
```
&SQL = CreateSQL("Select %Current(EFFDT) from
%Table(PSU_INSTR_TBL)");
```

Correct Answer: C

QUESTION 94

View the Exhibit.

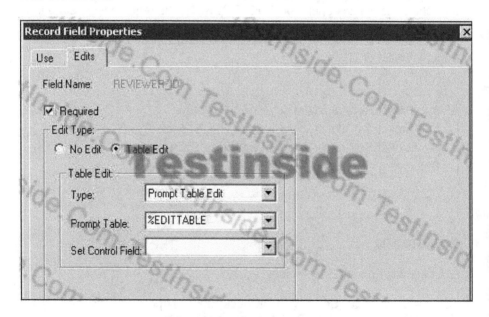

Note the Prompt Table field. Select the correct statement.
A. %EDITTABLE allows a user to override standard system edits.
B. %EDITTABLE allows the user select a prompt table at run time.
C. %EDITTABLE is used to assign a prompt table based on a value in another field on the page.
D. %EDITTABLE is meta-SQL that is used to filter prompt table values based

on run-time values.

E. %EDITTABLE is a system variable that resolves to a language-specific translate table at run time.

Correct Answer: C

QUESTION 95

You are testing a new asynchronous service operation to send employee job data to another system; however, no operation instance is created. Select three possible causes. (Choose three.)

A. The sending node is paused.
B. The sending domain is not active.
C. No Publication PeopleCode exists.
D. Publication PeopleCode is incorrect.
E. No outbound routings exist for the service operation.
F. The service operation is not active on the receiving system.

Correct Answer: CDE

QUESTION 96

View the Exhibit.

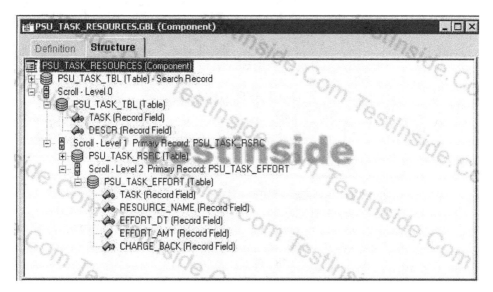

This PeopleCode program disables the CHARGE_BACK field:

```
Local Row &Row; &Row = GetRow();
&Row.PSU_TASK_EFFORT.CHARGE_BACK.Enabled = False;
```

For this program to work as shown, what is the highest level at which it could be placed?

A. PSU_TASK_TBL (Table)
B. PSU_TASK_RSRC (Table)
C. PSU_TASK_EFFORT (Table)
D. CHARGE_BACK (Record Field)
E. PSU_TASK_RESOURCES (Component)
F. PSU_TASK_TBL (Table) - Search Record

Correct Answer: C

QUESTION 97

The Application Engine program PSU_PROC_ORD uses values from PS_PSU_ORDER_DTL and PS_PSU_STOCK_TBL to update PS_PSU_STOCK_TBL.

You used a Do Select action to select QTY_ON_HAND, QTY_ORDERED, and ITEM_CD from PS_PSU_ORDER_DTL into the state record.
You added a SQL action to update PS_PSU_STOCK_TBL using the values in the state record. Which code would you use in the SQL action?

A. UPDATE PS_PSU_STOCK_TBL SET QTY_ON_HAND = %1 - %2 WHERE
    ITEM_CD = %3
    (QTY_ON_HAND, QTY_ORDERED, ITEM_CD)
B. %UPDATE (QTY_ON_HAND)
    SELECT QTY_ON_HAND - QTY_ORDERED FROM PS_PSU_STOCK_TBL
    WHERE ITEM_CD = %Bind(ITEM_CD)
C. UPDATE PS_PSU_STOCK_TBL
    SET QTY_ON_HAND = %Bind(QTY_ON_HAND) - %Bind(QTY_ORDERED)
    WHERE ITEM_CD = %Bind(ITEM_CD)
D. UPDATE PS_PSU_STOCK_TBL
    SET QTY_ON_HAND = Bind(QTY_ON_HAND) - Bind(QTY_ORDERED)
    WHERE ITEM_CD = Bind(ITEM_CD)
E. %UPDATE PS_PSU_STOCK_TBL
    SET QTY_ON_HAND = %QTY_ON_HAND - %QTY_ORDERED) WHERE
    ITEM_CD = %ITEM_CD

Correct Answer: C

QUESTION 98

View the Exhibit, which shows the WS Security page for the BPEL node definition.

You have consumed a Web service from the node BPEL that requires WS Security. On the Node Definitions page, you have entered PTTOOLS as the default user ID, DEMO as the external user ID, and DEMO as the external user password.

Based on this configuration, which user ID and password will be included in the SOAP header?

A. No SOAP header is added
B. DEMO as the user ID and no password
C. PTTOOLS as the user ID and no password
D. DEMO as the user ID and DEMO as the password
E. PTTOOLS as the user ID and PTTOOLS as the password

Correct Answer: D

QUESTION 99

View the Exhibit, which displays your file layout for a purchase order. In your application engine program to export the data to a file, which statement will instantiate the rowset?

A. &rowset=CreateRowset(Record.PSU_PO_HDR),CreateRowset(Record.PS
   U_PO_DTL);
B. &rowset=CreateRowset(Record.PSU_PO_HDR,CreateRowset(Record.PSU
   _PO_DTL));
C. &rowset1=CreateRowset(Record.PSU_PO_HDR);&rowset2=CreateRowset(
   Record.PSU_PO_DTL);
D. &MYFILE.SetFileLayout(FileLayout.PO_FILE);
E. &MYFILE = GetFile("E:\temp\PO_OUT.txt", "W", %FilePath_Absolute);

Correct Answer: B

QUESTION 100

All synchronous service operations in the messaging system with a status

of Done

A. All asynchronous service operations in the messaging system with a status of Done or Cancel

B. All synchronous and asynchronous service operations in the messaging system with a status of Error

C. Only asynchronous and synchronous service operations in the messaging system with a status of Done or Cancel

D. All asynchronous service operations in the messaging system with a status of Done or Cancel. In addition, the system will delete all synchronous service operations.

Correct Answer: E

QUESTION 101

You created a component interface and now must implement it on an online component. You drag the component interface into the PeopleCode event to generate the template.

This particular component interface is used to allow the GET method without data modification. Which two steps are required to modify the generated PeopleCode component interface template for implementing the GET Method without data modification? (Choose two.)

A. Uncomment the Save and Cancel methods.
B. Set the component interface Get/Create keys.
C. Modify the PeopleCode by substituting values for [*].
D. Uncomment the Create section and comment out the Get section.
E. Modify the template to assign values to the other component interface properties.

Correct Answer: BC

QUESTION 102

In the PeopleCode Debugger, how do you examine the structure and contents of the component buffer?

A. Select View, Component Buffers.
B. Select View, Component Processor.
C. Select Debug > View Component Buffers.
D. Select Debug > View Component Structure.
E. Click the Structure tab on the component definition.
F. Insert a Display Component Buffers; statement in your PeopleCode program.

Correct Answer: C

www.ingramcontent.com/pod-product-compliance
Lightning Source LLC
LaVergne TN
LVHW051616050326
832903LV00033B/4521